100 Animals For Toddler
Coloring Book Vol.1

Easy Coloring Books for Toddlers

Belongs to:

_____

_____

Ellie and Friends

100 Animals For Toddler

Coloring Book Vol. 1

Copyright: Published in the United States by Ellie and Friends
Published January 2020

Test your colors

100 ANIMALS FOR TODDLER COLORING BOOK

This is Volume 1

PUPPY

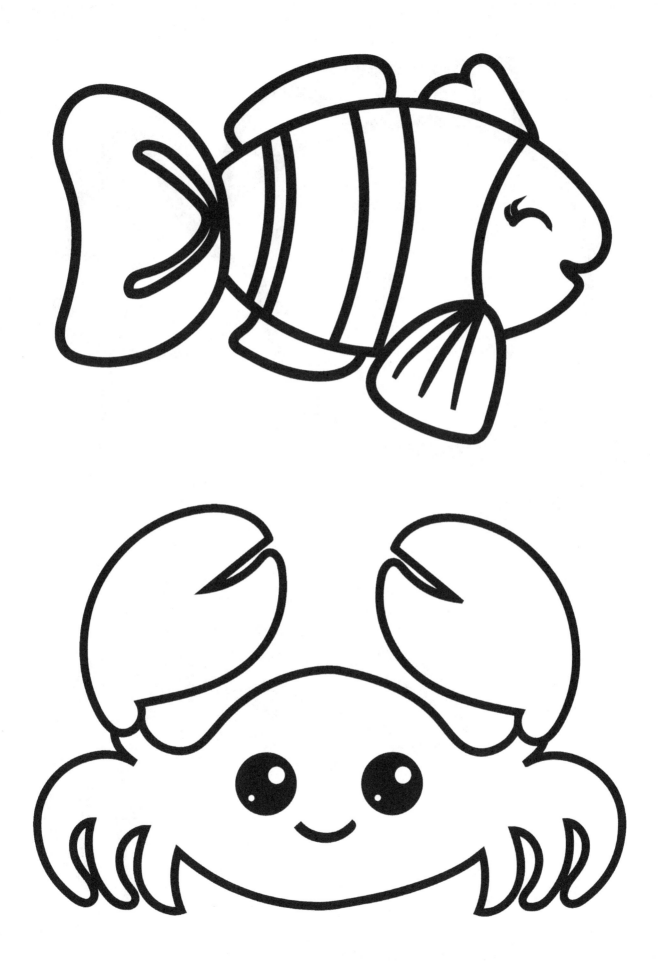

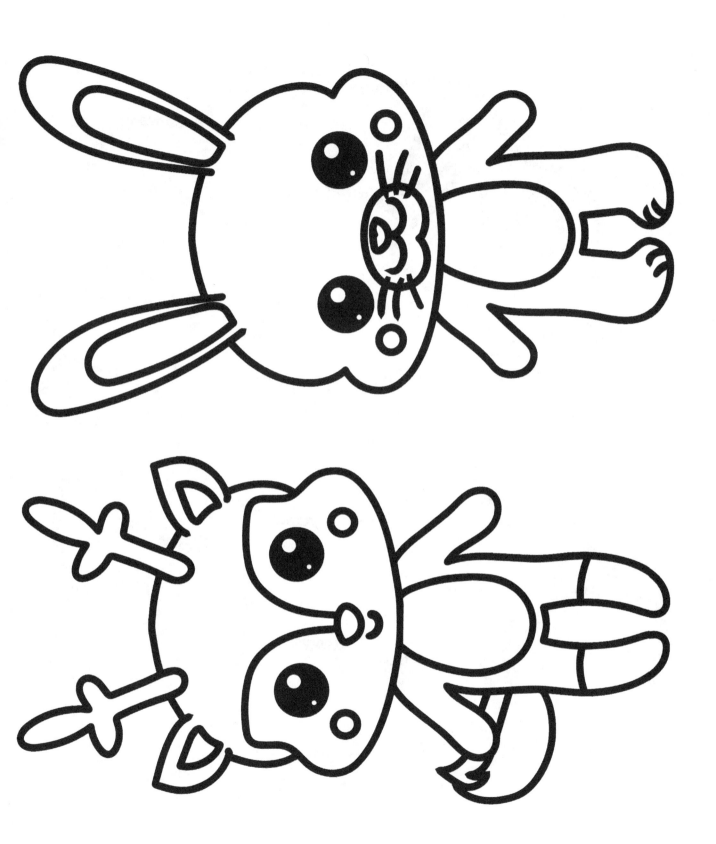

Made in the USA
Middletown, DE
19 December 2020